THE EDDIE FUTCH INTERVIEW

A Conversation with Boxing Legend
and Trainer of Champions

By

F. Daniel Somrack

For

Adriana Hernandez Jimenez

Copyright © by F. Daniel Somrack/BoxingScribeBooks September 2017

ALL RIGHTS RESERVED. No part of this book may be reproduced or transmitted in any form by any means, electronic or mechanical, including photocopying and recording, or by any information storage and retrieval system, except as may be expressly permitted in writing from the author. All images © F. Daniel Somrack

TABLE OF CONTENTS

Part I 5
   Preface 6
   Introduction 9
   The Eddie Futch Interview: Las Vegas, Nevada, June 1993 11

Part II 36
   Brewster Center 37
   Joe Louis 38
   Jack Blackburn 39
   Ray Arcel 40
   Jimmy Edgar 41
   Holman Williams 42
   Charley Burley 43
   Henry Armstrong 44
   Barry Gordy 46
   Don Jordon 47
   Ali v. Frazier: "Fight of the Century" 48
   Ali v. Frazier III: "Thrilla in Manila" 49
   Joe Frazier 51
   Joe Frazier v. George Foreman 52
   Ken Norton 53
   Alexis Arguello 55
   Bobby Chacon 57
   Ruben Olivares 59
   Larry Holmes v. Michael Spinks 61
   Riddick Bowe 62
   Evander Holyfield v. Lennox Lewis 63

Lennox Lewis v. Riddick Bowe 64
George Foreman vs. Tommy Morrison................................65
Tommy "The Duke" Morrison...66
"Iron" Mike Tyson..67
About the Author 69

Part I

Preface

As a filmmaker, I had the opportunity to work with "the greatest" Muhammad Ali on the best-selling, sports documentary, *Champions Forever*. In 1988, our production company ION Pictures brought Muhammad Ali and his ring rivals Joe Frazier, George Foreman, Ken Norton and Larry Holmes to Las Vegas, Nevada for in-depth interviews covering their amateur and professional boxing careers.

Four of these great champions including Frazier, Foreman, Holmes and Norton had one thing in common. They had all faced off against Muhammad Ali with three of the fighters, Joe Frazier, Ken Norton and Larry Holmes having had the unique distinction of defeating Ali in the ring. It wasn't a coincidence. They had all been guided to victory by the same man - master trainer, Eddie Futch.

As the Story Consultant on *Champion Forever*, I was always curious about the strategy employed by Mr. Futch that allowed his disciples to defeat Ali. The only way to solve that mystery was to speak to the man directly. In 1993, my co-writer Geoff Strain and I traveled to Las Vegas, Nevada, to do just that. Our objective was to film a full retrospective with Mr. Futch; highlighting the key moments of his storied career in the sport.

For over six decades, the venerable Eddie Futch had been guiding the professional boxing careers of hundreds of fighters, creating over twenty world champions. Mr. Futch had the unique ability to impart his deep understanding of the sport while consistently instilling in his fighters a winning philosophy that made him a 1993 inductee into the International Boxing Hall of Fame.

During the course of this following interview, Futch spoke candidly about his unique ability to assess an opponent's strengths and weaknesses and capitalize on them. He explained the customized training regime he employed with his fighters that gave them a marked advantage over their opponents. His system resulted in some of the biggest upsets in boxing history.

The Futch method was also responsible for Muhammad Ali's first two defeats. Having Joe Frazier, adopt a bob-and-weave style, beat Ali in the 1971 "Fight of the Century." His instructions for Ken Norton to, "jab when Ali jabbed," offset Ali's rhythm and allowed for Norton to land his jaw-breaking blow and gain a split-decision victory over Ali in 1973.

During our interview, the 82-year-old trainer highlighted his contributions to other great fights of the century. He gave a truthful assessment of the "Thrilla in Manila" bout, and the reason behind his fourteenth round stoppage. He recapped his strategy for Alexis Arguello to defeat the unbeaten Ray "Boom Boom" Mancini and the controversy surrounding Arguello's loss to Aaron Pryor. He also gave his honest assessment of the top heavyweight contenders of 1993.

It was an honor to spend a few hours in the presence of this elder statesman of boxing. His historical knowledge was second to none. With alacrity and deep insight, Mr. Futch recalled in chronological order, the highlights of his career in the game beginning as an amateur boxer in the 1930s. From the "Brown Bomber," Joe Louis, to Riddick "Big Daddy" Bowe, Eddie Futch had, in one way or another, touched the lives of everyone involved in the sport for over sixty years.

The undefeated Bowe would be the last heavyweight champion under his tutelage, although he would continue training fighters until his retirement in 1998. He remained in Las Vegas, living comfortably with his wife Eva, until he passed away in October 2011.

After completing this following 40-minute interview, the tape was shelved and never seen and/or used for any personal or commercial purposes. Recently discovered languishing in a storage unit, I made a written transcription of our one-on-one conversation exactly as it was recorded.

In Part II. of this book, I expand upon and clarify certain references made during the interview. I've also included additional background information on the individuals mentioned in the transcription and reported the eventual outcome of the fights of 1993 that Mr. Futch alluded to in the show. Also included are photographs of the Hall of Fame champions who are part of the Eddie Futch legacy.

F. Daniel Somrack
Los Angeles, California

Introduction

Born to tenant farmers in Hillsboro, Mississippi, on August 9, 1911, Eddie Futch relocated with his family to Detroit when he was five years old. When his parents separated three years later, Eddie took over the responsibility of raising his younger brother and sister while his mother worked as a maid and housekeeper.

In his teens, Futch was a stand-out basketball player and joined a semi-pro club called the Moreland Flashes. In 1927, he played against the Savoy Big Five out of Chicago, a team that later became known as The Harlem Globetrotters.

Marriage and the stock market crash of 1929 ended Futch's dream of a college education and a professional basketball career. Circumstances forced him to take a job working as a waiter for $15 a week at the Wolverine Hotel in downtown Detroit.

Exercising at the YMCA to stay in shape, Futch was prompted by a good friend to join the Brewster Recreation Center where he was introduced to boxing. A quick study, Futch went on to win the club championship and the 1933 Detroit Lightweight Golden Gloves title as well.

During this time, Eddie befriended the "Brown Bomber," Joe Louis, who was also a member of the Brewster team. Louis asked the smaller Futch to be his sparring partner to help him increase his timing and speed. Louis believed that if he developed enough quickness to catch an elusive lightweight, he would have marked advantage when fighting much slower heavyweights.

After his Golden Gloves career, Futch was sidelined from a professional boxing with a heart condition. He turned his talents to training fighters in the early 1940s. He helped develop some of the top prospects of that era including Luther Burgess, Lester Felton and Jimmy Edgar.

Futch also trained a young man named Berry Gordy during this time. Gordy, a promising bantamweight, would later find his niche in record producing by founding his own music label called Motown Records. Gordy would later attribute his success at Motown to the principles taught to him by Eddie Futch.

Another decade would pass before Futch's skill and tenacity as a trainer would be recognized on the world stage. In 1958, Don Jordan, with only 16 months under Futch's tutelage, became the first of his many world champions.

Throughout his distinguished career, Futch would be associated with some of the greatest prize-fighters of his Twentieth Century including Smokin' Joe Frazier, Alexis Arguello, Larry Holmes, Ken Norton, Bob Foster, Bobby Chacon, Riddick Bowe and Michael Spinks.

The Eddie Futch Interview: Las Vegas, Nevada, June 1993

1). You started boxing at the Brewster Center in Detroit, and you were a quick study. In 1933 you won the Golden Gloves Championship. Can you describe the competition in that era?

The competition was quite good at that time. We had a number of promising young fighters, and in that group was a young man who was competing for various Golden Gloves titles. The young man was named Joe Louis.

2). As an amateur, you sparred a lot with Joe Louis, and I read where you found a flaw in his style and you were able to capitalize on it with a short left hook.

Yes. In working with Joe Louis, I found out you had to be very precise with every movement you made because he had such fast hands. I used to sit outside the ring at times when I wasn't sparring with him and study every move he made. In this way, I was able to avoid being hit with one of those terrific left hooks that he threw.

3). He seemed to throw punches real short, but still, he had so much power on them. Was it the way he put his body into them?

Yes. He put his body into almost every shot he threw, and that was how he was able to have such great power with even his short shots.

4). Can you comment on Jack Blackburn?

A great trainer... great trainer. He came along at a time when a man of color had to be exceptional to command the respect and the attention he got from the fighter he had. I was fortunate enough to have been around him enough to absorb some of the knowledge that he was capable of demonstrating.

5). How about Ray Arcel?

Ray Arcel was another one. Of all the trainers around New York, when I first went to New York in the early 40s, and I looked at all of them, and I could just tell just how much they knew by watching. Having been involved with people like Joe Louis and Holman Williams and others with sound boxing principles, Ray Arcel was the only one I thought I could learn something from.

6). Can you talk a little bit about some of your early fighters like Lester Felton, Luther Burgess and Jimmy Edgar?

Lester Felton, Jimmy Edgar and Luther Burgess were the tops in their division. In those days, it was little harder to get title shots for fighters of their caliber because boxing was very tightly controlled by certain elements. Fighters in their ilk had to wait for long periods of time to get the kind of exposure that would take him right to the top.

7). Did Sugar Ray Robinson ever fight Jimmy Edgar?

No, they never fought. They sparred a lot together because they both were on the Joe Louis Tour during World War II. They never fought each other, although they were signed to fight once. Robinson had made a blank statement to a promoter in Chicago that he would fight anybody within the radius of 300 miles of Chicago, anybody. He forgot that Jimmy Edgar was within a radius of 300 miles.

So the promoter said, "I got him." He said, "I got his agreement." When Robinson found out that he was expected to fight Edgar, he just disregarded the agreement altogether.

They fought each other time after time on the tour. There were three welterweights on the Joe Louis Tour. Robinson, Edgar and Jackie Wilson. So they would mix it up. Robinson would box Jackie Wilson one day, then Edgar the next day; then he would have a day off. Then Edgar and Wilson would box each other in a round-robin like that. Then they had the heavyweights Joe Louis, George Nicholson and someone else.

8). Tell me something about Holman Williams. He was one of the great middleweights of the 1940s.

For pure boxer, he was the best I'd ever seen. A pure boxer, he wasn't a puncher. He'd box the punchers. He beat guys like Archie Moore in his last year fighting.

9). Williams had a rising jab. What was it?

Well, he had about four different jabs. The rising jab would start about body level and come up. If you were coming in, it was like walking into a pole somebody had stuck out. It took perfect timing for that maneuver. I saw him use it against Jake LaMotta. LaMotta got the decision, but I don't see what the judges were thinking about.

10). Did Holman Williams ever get a shot at the title?

No. He never got a shot at the title.

11). How about Charlie Burley?

It's Charlie Burley when you talk about all-around fighters who could box and punch. He could do it all and never got a shot of the title.

12). Why weren't these guys given shots of the title?

Because of the way boxing was structured in those days. Certain people got shots, and certain people didn't get shots. Archie Moore was a rated fighter ten years before he got his shot. Archie Moore turned pro in 1936, the year that I quit, and he got his title shot in 1952.

13). Did Charlie Burley ever fight Sugar Ray Robinson? If not, was it intentional?

No, they never fought, and yes, it was intentional. Let me tell you a story. Walter Winchell had done some favors for Robinson, and Robinson had made some free contributions to his "cancer fund" so they were pretty close. So one day Walter Winchell says to Robinson, "Ray why don't you fight Charlie Burley?" Ray's answer was, "Walter, I thought you were my friend." [laughs]

14). You helped Charlie Burley get elected into the Boxing Hall of Fame.

Right. I worked one fight against Charlie Burley with Holman Williams. That was a classic. It was at Soldiers Field in Cincinnati in '42. Burley won that fight, but they fought seven times. Nobody wanted to fight Burley once, and Williams fought him seven times, and they split even. Burley won three and Williams won three, and one was called a "no-contest" because they were doing anything out there.

They had fought each other so many times, and each man knew what the other fellow was going to do, so they couldn't do much. Burley had the edge because he knocked Williams out once in his three wins, and Holman had defeated him by decision in each of the three times that he won.

Burley had knocked out J.D. Turner, the fellow who had fought Billy Conn two fights after Conn lost to Louis. Turner went the distance with Conn. Burley at 152 pounds knocked out Turner who weighed 215. I asked Turner, and I'm not getting this from anyone else, I asked Turner when he was the referee for a flight I had down in Texas. I used to have a fighter named Paul Andrews who boxed in Texas, and J.D. Turner was the referee.

So after the fight I asked Turner, "How much did you weigh the night you fought Charlie Burley?" He laughed and said, "I weighed 218 pounds and that little sucker hit me with a left hook in the sixth round, and I woke up in the dressing room." [laughs]

15). How about Henry Armstrong?

Henry Armstrong was phenomenal, phenomenal. Anytime you have a featherweight fight for the middleweight title, you got something that you'll

never see again. He won the featherweight title, then he skipped over the lightweight title and went for the welterweight championship and won that from Barney Ross. Then went back down to the lightweight division and won that title. Then went back up again to challenge for the middleweight crown and fought to a draw. If the judges had been on the money that night, we would have had one man holding four titles simultaneously.

He would've held the featherweight, lightweight, welterweight and middleweight championships. Phenomenal man. The first time I saw him he was fighting a Canadian named Patsy Drouillard. I heard about how many punches he threw and the pace he set, and Drouillard was the same type of fighter that Armstrong was; he threw a lot of punches too.

For the first three rounds, they were pretty busy rounds. These two guys really went after it. And in the fourth round, Drouillard stepped up the pace, and Armstrong doubled it, and out of there went Drouillard. [laughs]. (Armstrong fought Orville Drouillard "The Windsor Whirlwind" (August 31, 1937) at Detroit Michigan winning by TKO in round five. Drouillard was trained by his uncle "Patsy" Drouillard.)

16). Berry Gordy, the former President and founder of Motown Records, attributes his success at Motown to Eddie Futch.

He has often told me that. When he comes to Las Vegas, and in fact in the earlier days before he sold Motown, he would come to Vegas often, and he would have one of his lieutenants find me. I'd be from one hotel to the other because I was training fighters who fought for various hotels. Berry would tell his lieutenants to get out and find me and have me come to the show. He told me that he had told all of his artists at Motown about the principles I taught him. He said that entertainment and boxing, they're all the same.

He'd say, "The things that Mr. Futch taught me are the things I'm teaching you about your careers." He always told me, he'd say, "You're famous at Motown. Everybody knows you."

17). You were in Mexico City in 1957 and there was an incident where there was a ref giving instructions to your opponent in Spanish, and you were able to understand what he said and counter those moves. Can you tell me about that?

Yes. That amused me a great deal because the ref had no idea I knew what he was saying. I was able to take advantage of the things he was saying because I could tell my fighter how to counter punch all the refs instructions.

18). Don Jordan was your first world champion. Where did you find Don Jordan?

Don Jordan was one of those fighters who trained in the gym in Los Angeles where I was training a couple of fighters that I had brought from Detroit. I had seen him fight on television once, and I thought he was the most promising young fighter on the West Coast.

I was amazed that he hadn't gotten any further than he had because of his ability. I thought he could be a world champion. I never thought that I would be associated with him because he belonged to a syndicate then that didn't like my style. So later I bumped into him in Mexico City.

He was having a bad time down there, and he wasn't being taken care of properly. He came to me to borrow some money. I gave him the money, and he didn't even know it was a gift, but I gave it to him anyway because I was leaving in a few hours, and I didn't want to see him left there with no money and in such a bad condition.

When I got back to the states, I talked to Jackie McCoy with whom I was very friendly with. I was managing and training a group of his fighters and I told him about Jordan's plight, and he wound up buying the [Jordan's] contract.

I have suggested that he buy the contract because, being in the condition he was in, they couldn't think very much of him, so you could probably get it very cheaply. So he bought the contract for $3500 and turned the fighter over to me to train, and twenty months later, Don Jordan was the Welterweight Champion of the World.

19). He upset Virgil Akins for the title?

Yes, Virgil Akins was champion at the time Jordan won the title.

20). How did you first begin training Joe Frazier?

Well, I had been working with my big stable of fighters in Detroit and was in the process of securing fights for them. I was back-and-forth a lot to Philadelphia. I'd sent a lot of my fighters to Philly and became very well acquainted with the boxing profession in that city.

My fighters always attracted a lot of attention among trainers and managers because of their style and ability, and so I became quite well-known in Philadelphia. Now, this was in the early 40s, 1942, '43, '44, and then later I moved to Los Angeles, California, in 1951.

When there was no one in Philadelphia, I was in Los Angeles. When all of the trainers and managers who had fighters that wanted to fight in Los Angeles, they would always bring them to me, and in many cases fighters that I had not known of, and managers I had not known of before, would be advised to see me if they came to Los Angeles to fight.

So Joe Frazier was one of the last of a long line of Philadelphia fighters who were sent to me, or brought to me, after I moved to Los Angeles. At the time, I was called by Yank Durham, Frazier's manager, about becoming Joe's trainer. I didn't know Yank at all, and I didn't know Joe. I knew of Joe through his Olympic Gold Medal.

In the years I was around Philadelphia, Yank was a soldier in the Army during World War II, and Joe Frazier was just a four-year-old kid in South Carolina, but they had heard about me.

After Joe had become old enough to fight, and Yank was out of the Army and managing fighters, they called me up and talked with me on the phone, and they liked what they heard, so Yank got on a plane with Joe and came out to Los Angeles. The minute I met them at the plane, we got an instant combination of chemistry that just worked, right from the start.

21). Muhammad Ali's title was vacated in '67, and there was a WBA tournament to fill the vacancy, and you kept Joe Frazier out of the tournament. Why did you keep him [Frazier] out of the tournament?

I reasoned first that if there were ten heavyweights in the world, and Joe being number two on the list, I don't remember who they rated number one at the time, Joe being number two on the list, he would be in the tournament.

They expected the first eight fighters on the W.B.A. list to be in the heavyweight tournament. So I advised Yank not to go in it. Yank had intended to go in because he thought it was an honor to be included in this heavyweight tournament to decide a champion. I said, "I wouldn't put him in the tournament." And Yank said, "Why do you think like that?'

I said, "Well, you're going to have to fight eight fighters in the tournament when you're going to come out of the tournament with one champion and seven losers. And the winner is going to have to fight at least three or four times to come out a champion. If you leave Joe out of the tournament, you will only have eight fighters in the tournament." Joe was one of the two who didn't go in; the other one was George Chuvalo.

"Then all we have to do is beat George Chuvalo and wait for the winner of the tournament. Because all of the ten eligible fighters will have to be accounted for then." Yank took my advice and kept Joe out of the tournament. Joe subsequently knocked out George Chuvalo, and Jimmy Ellis came out of the tournament the winner.

22). What was your strategy for Joe Frazier in the March 1971 "Fight of the Century" against Muhammad Ali? What was your strategy for Joe?

My strategy was pressure. Joe was a lot shorter than Muhammad Ali, so I had developed Joe into a bobbing and weaving fighter. In fact, I did that after the Oscar Bonavena fight in which he got knocked down a couple times being a standup fighter and walking in. So I developed a bobbing and weaving style for Frazier, and we used it to great effect against Muhammad Ali.

Ali had never fought a fighter who had that style, and I made Joe concentrate on body punching because that [the body] presented a bigger target, and it had a weakening effect on an opponent. I made him keep the pressure on and punch to the body and make Ali bring his hands down and take away his punching.

The constant pressure put on him against the ropes and in the corners where it was easy to find him and ignore the head until Ali began to bend forward, putting his elbows around the body to prevent the body punches from landing. Then the head would come forward, and Frazier could go after it. That strategy worked perfect against Ali.

23). Your corner was always cool compared to Ali's where there was so much commotion going on. Was that conscious? Did you always try to keep everything cool?

Yes, that was part of my style. I want fighters to be completely relaxed. I don't want them to feel that I'm excited, to make them feel that everything is under control, and consequently that makes it easier for him to work in a relaxed manner.

24). I wanted to ask you about the fight with Joe Frazier and Muhammad Ali in Manila. You stopped the fighting the fourteenth round when Joe's eye was closed.

Right. The left eye was completely closed, and the right eye was closing fast. I had to alter my strategy fast in that fight because of the sight problem. Up till the tenth round, I thought it was going to be a resounding victory for Joe. In fact, Ali wanted to get out of there at the end of the tenth round, but Angelo insisted on him staying in and following his plan.

Swelling started in the eleventh round, and it became quite noticeable in the twelfth. The left eye started closing fast, and at the end of the twelfth round, he could barely see out of that left eye, so I had to move him back about six to eight inches from Ali.

Instead of being right on top of them, because being low and in close, he couldn't see Ali's hands with the eye partly closed, so I moved him back about eight inches and made him stand up a little straighter which was right in the target range. That's the only place he could see, the only position from which he could see.

Ali noticed right away because he's a great opportunist, and he started firing the right-hand, and he caught Joe repeatedly with it--with the right hand on that damaged eye. Some of the shots started the swelling to increase in the right eye also. So I thought, "Well, Ali's throwing a lot of punches, and it's late in the fight. Perhaps he'll punch himself out and slow the pace down."

Besides getting his good shots off first, Ali knew this was his opportunity, and he kept firing. He hit Joe in the thirteenth around with a straight hand that knocked his mouthpiece six rows out into the audience.

I said, "He just can't keep that pace up," so I sent Joe out for the fourteenth round, but Ali kept up that pace right from the start of the fourteenth round. I turned to George Benton, who is my assistant for a number of years, and I said, "George, after this round I'm stopping the fight," and George said, "I think it's a good decision."

So when Joe came back to the corner after the fourteenth round, and Ali, he had never slowed his pace of throwing that right hand, and when Joe sat down and I told him, "Joe, it's all over; I'm stopping the fight.'" He jumped up, and I touched him on the shoulder and said, "Sit down, Joe. It's over." So he sat down. I went over and got Padilla, Carlos Padilla, the referee, and told him that I wasn't going to let Joe come out for the fifteenth round.

25). Joe Frazier fought George Foreman in Jamaica where he [Frazier] lost his heavyweight championship. His new style didn't work against George Foreman. Why didn't it work?

Well, I'll give you an example why it didn't work. Yank Durham would always like me to come to training camp a week or so after the camp had opened. He said, "You always bring a fresh perspective, and you can see things that we can't see although we're here." So I came in the usual week to ten days later into the camp in Jamaica, and what I saw horrified me.

I told Yank, "This is not a training camp. This is just one great big party." This was the winter time, and all the jetsetters from New York and Philadelphia were there, and they were having a big party at the hotel where the training was actually being carried out, around the pool and here and there. Joe Frazier got caught up in it, although he was going through his rigorous training schedule; his mind was on the party.

And so I said, "Yank, this is bad." Ken Norton at the time had been working with Frazier as a sparring partner for three years. I was handling his career also, and so I had Norton spar with Frazier the first day that I got in, and I was surprised with what I saw. Then I had him spar the second day so I could confirm what I thought I saw, and sure enough, it didn't go well.

So I called Norton aside after the workout and said, "Ken, I can see what's going on outside the ring from my point of view, but what's going on inside that perhaps I can't see?" He says, "Joe seems to have lost his drive." Well, Norton was getting the best of the workouts for the first time in three and a half years.

I said, "Okay. You're not working anymore." So Norton had a good two-week vacation in Nassau. He was legitimately in the party, but what Norton said turned out to be very true. What I had said to Yank when I first saw the camp, I said, "Joe is caught up in all of this partying." I said, "Regardless of the fact that he is just going through the motions training, it's just not there, Yank." Sure enough, it was the worst fight of his career.

26). You had two fighters who were able to defeat Muhammad Ali: Ken Norton and Joe Frazier. Ken Norton's style was completely different from Joe Frazier's. What was your strategy for Ken Norton to defeat Muhammad Ali?

Well, I had picked some of the other things about Muhammad Ali besides the things that I had noticed when he fought Frazier and some of the other fighters he had been successful with. He got away with a lot of things that were not good boxing moves because of his speed and his daring. He did things that weren't good boxing, but he got away with them and looked sensational doing it.

Ali would carry his right hand too far to the right when he was jabbing, and the right hand belongs right in front of the face when you're jabbing. With his speed and daring-do, he could carry his right hand out here and get away with it. And when his opponents tried to make him miss the jab by slipping and counterpunching, he was too quick; he was gone.

If you tried to duck and come up and counterpunch, it was too late, Ali's gone. So I told Ken Norton, "You're as tall as Ali is, and you've got a good jab. When he jabs, I want you to jab the same time. Don't try to slip him and counterpunch. You go with him because your right hand is going to be here, and his right hand is going to be over there, and you're both making the same moves, and your left jab will go down the center and hit him right in the face, and his will miss because your left hand, in traveling to his face, will cross his left hand."

"In other words, what I want you to do is, when he punches, you punch at the same time. Don't try to make a miss. You just go right to him and punch." This simple maneuver so disturbed Ali's overall plan because without his jab, he was left with nothing else to do but go defensive. So Norton, with that simple move, was able to untrack Ali.

27). In what round do you think that Muhammad Ali's jaw was broken?

They claim the second. I claim the eleventh because with as many right-hands that he got hit with after the second round--the round in which they claim he got the injury--with that number of right hands he got hit with--that jaw would have been in fragments.

28). Alexis Arguello was another one of your fighters.

Alexis and I had quite a career together. I enjoyed working with Alexis because he was a consummate professional. He beat the greatest fighters in his division, and in the divisions he moved up into. He beat the best fighters in the world because he was so solid. He did things in such a professional way that he would wear them down.

If you notice his record, it indicates that he beat the best fighters in the world in the late rounds. He knocked them out in the thirteenth and the fourteenth rounds. The best names on his record were the ones he beat that late because he had a very solid program right from the start. He did the right things and got the right results in the end.

29). What was your strategy for Arguello to beat Ray "Boom Boom" Mancini?

That was a classic fight. "Boom Boom Mancini," as I told Alexis Arguello, "is undefeated. This young fighter has been all successful. The name Alexis Arguello means absolutely nothing to him. You're just another opponent as far as he's concerned. So he's going to come after you the same way he would anyone else.

"He's in the hands of a good trainer, Murphy Griffith, who used to be my assistant, and he's going to be in top physical condition because Murphy is a real taskmaster in getting his fighters in shape. So in the early part of the fight, he's going to be ahead because he's going to start fast. I want you to start faster than you usually do, but you still won't be able to match his speed.

"With his quickness, he'll get inside of your jab and when he gets to you, or within your range, he's going to hit you with lead-off punches. I want you to counterpunch, but with every counter, I want you to throw to the body and forget about the head altogether. I want you to throw those shots to the body to take away some of that stress, but it's going to take time. It's going to take five or six rounds before it starts to work.

"When it cues in about the sixth or seventh round, he will be coming slow enough from the effect of the body punching to make your jab start to work, and you'll start hitting him cleanly, catching him coming in, and when that starts to happen the fight is practically over. It will turn around completely." This happened in the eighth round, and from then on it was an Arguello show.

30). What happened in the Aaron Pryor fight? Was it Arguello moving up in weight and not being able to carry the strength with him?

No. Alexis Arguello was Alexis that night. And if anyone noticed how tough the flight was up until the fourteenth round, the round which Pryor had been sent out after his corner had mentioned a specific bottle that they wanted him to drink from. After that hard thirteen rounds of work between these two fighters, Pryor came out of his corner after sipping from this bottle as if it were the first round.

And that I think is what made the difference in the fight. Not only was he revitalized from whatever the contents of that bottle was, but it had to be discouraging to Alexis to know that after coming out with so much steam, and so much firepower after that hard thirteen rounds they had fought previously, he had to feel in his mind that there was something wrong.

At that time, he didn't know what it was, and none of us knew exactly what it was but I suspected something. Now, there was an eleven-man commission in Florida at that time, a boxing commission, and there were no drug tests administered. In all of the confusion that surrounded the end of that flight, the commission completely forgot to test for drugs.

31). You worked with Bobby Chacon.

I worked with Bobby for about a year. I know he had about seven or eight fights with me, and he had lost two previous flights to Ruben Olivares, and he had been stopped in both of them. I took over his training, and after about four or five fights with me, he boxed Olivares again and won a ten-round decision over him.

32). Olivares was a great fighter.

Right. What a fighter he was.

33). Your strategy for Michael Spinks against Larry Holmes?

I didn't work that fight. I trained both fighters, and my excuse for not working the flight was, or my reason was, because both men were going for special places in boxing history.

Michael was undefeated as a light-heavyweight and the undisputed light-heavyweight champion. He had never lost a fight and wanted to be the first light-heavyweight champion to win the heavyweight championship. Larry Holmes was undefeated and going for a special place in history too. He wanted to be the first heavyweight champion to retire with more wins than Rocky Marciano, and he was within two fights of that position.

So I said to the press when they asked me who I was going to work with after the fight was signed, I said, "Neither one." They said "Why?" I said, "Because I train both fighters. Because they're both going for special places in boxing history."

I said that I could not, in all good conscience, contribute to the defeat of either man, so I stepped aside. Although I passed up an enormous purse, there are certain things in life that I treasure more.

34). You are currently training Heavyweight Champion of the World Riddick Bowe. How do you think Riddick Bowe would fare against Mike Tyson?

I think he would fare against Mike Tyson the same way that Buster Douglas fared against Mike Tyson because he has the same equipment, and he's younger and punches harder.

I predicted the Douglas win over Tyson three years before it happened. I'd seen Tyson box four different tall men, and although he won in each instance, he had trouble with tall man. He had trouble with men who could box, tall men who had good mobility and a good left hand, and Buster Douglas had all of those things.

A tall man who was smart enough to set the locale of the action. He boxed him on the outside, stayed off the ropes and out of the corners, and tied them up on the inside, and beat him. Bowe can do all of that.

35). What attributes do you look for in a fighter?

Well, first of all, physically, I want him to have good reflexes. I want him to have good balance. I want him to have a real desire. See if he's got that. Those are the basic things you should have if you want to be a good fighter. Then you can be a puncher, or you can be a boxer. You could be a combination of the two, but you got to have balance. You got to have good reflexes, coordination and desire. Desire is the flame.

36). Do you ask your fighters that? Why they want to box?

I ask them questions, and they don't know what I'm after. Bowe didn't know what I was after when I met him. I asked Rock Newman to send him up to Reno. Rock called me from D.C. He had seen that I turned Bowe down from Butch Lewis. I had turned him down after Butch Lewis called me about Bowe.

I hadn't been able to watch the amateurs for a long time because I had three world champions at the time: McCallum, Hill and Starling. I hadn't been able to watch amateurs at all, so I didn't know anything about Bowe.

I had heard all of these disparaging comments after his Olympic loss to Lennox Lewis, and they went into things, reasons why he lost. He wouldn't do this; he wouldn't do that.

So I said, "Well, at my age," I was seventy-eight at the time, that "I don't have time to waste with a fighter, or with anybody, that's going to waste my time. I have no interest." That's why I turned him down from Butch Lewis. Then Jon Sacreceno wrote in USA Today about my refusal to take Bowe, and Rock Newman read it and called me from D.C.

I was in Reno, and he talked for half an hour. He said a few things that caught my attention, or said some things that he thought would catch my attention, and there were carrots in it that I listened for or I picked out of all the things he was saying. I said, "Why don't you send the kid up to me and let me talk to him personally?"

So he got a hold of Bowe and sent him up to Reno. So I sat down and talked with Bowe and asked him a lot of questions. I had a little drill and tested his reflexes, and I was amazed at how good they were. He didn't know what I was doing then either. I've felt him out real casual and asked him questions or just listened to what he had to say. I decided this has been a much-maligned kid, and I thought, "Gees, this is not the person that I was led to believe he was," and so I decided to give him a chance.

Everybody thinks that because he's six-five and 230 pounds and just turning 21 years old, they think that he's a man. This is a teenager. This is a boy, and he's acting like a boy. He's acting like a boy, and he's in the frame of the big man, so everyone thinks he's a flake.

37). Evander Holyfield?

Evander Holyfield is a well conditioned, well disciplined fighter. I saw him on the TV show last night, [Up Close] when he and Bowe were on the same show at the same time. He's got a big heart. He takes a fairly good punch, although I've seen him hurt more lately than he was in earlier fights.

Bowe had him badly hurt, and the Bowe of today would've stopped him. November 13, [1992] after he got him into that big trouble in the tenth round, he would of stopped him. He was a little over anxious, but now he's more deliberate. Evander Holyfield will give anybody in the division a tough fight and will beat most of them. He'll beat Lennox Lewis if Lewis takes that fight.

He'll never get to Bowe because Holyfield will beat him. He'll be on top of him, and Lennox Lewis doesn't fight very good going back, and he'll be going back when he is fighting Holyfield, looking for punching room, and Holyfield will be right there in his face. He takes a good punch and comes right back.

38). What is your opinion of Lennox Lewis?

Lennox Lewis, in his last fight, showed some of the things I had been wondering about. I threw the Razor Ruddick fight out altogether because Ruddick didn't look like himself at all before the fight.

39). Do you see any weaknesses in Lewis's style?

Yes, I do. I see definite weaknesses and we will go right after them.

40). What is your opinion of Tommy Morrison?

Tommy Morrison is a good puncher and seemed to be in very good shape the other night against Foreman. He's got a good left hook that he can depend on. But, if you set your sights on beating the hook, you have Tommy Morrison beaten.

He's come up the hard way. He fought some tough fights coming up, like Joe Hipp and some of those others like Carl Williams was a hard fight for him. He got off the floor a couple times in that fight. He has potential, and he showed it against Foreman, that if he could keep his mind set on boxing, and not try to knock his man out with every shot, that he could be more effective.

41). He seemed to frustrate George Foreman by moving his head so much, not allowing him a target.

Yes, but one thing I noticed and wondered about is when George would back him into a corner, and he still wouldn't throw.

42). Do you think Mike Tyson will fight again?

Yes. I think Mike Tyson will be back. I think he'll be back

43). Mike Tyson is in exile in his prime years the same way Muhammad Ali was in exile in his prime.

Mike Tyson depends on his physical attributes where Muhammad Ali depended on his knowledge and his skills. Tyson depends on his power and his sharpness, his natural and physical sharpness.

When that starts to decline... sometimes it can only be measured by the results. A fellow seems to be doing the same thing, and actually he is doing the same thing that he was doing when he was at his peak, but they're slower, and the only way you can measure the difference in the speed by which the reflexes react is when you see him getting hit with punches that he couldn't have been hit with before. You see him missing punches he wouldn't have missed before, they know he's slowing up. But physically, he looks the same.

44). Do you have any words of wisdom about life for young men?

Be your own man. If I hadn't followed my own instincts against what others wanted to me to do, I wouldn't be sitting here with you today.

45). How would you like to be remembered?

As a man who did the best he could with what he had to work with.

Part II

Brewster Center

Opened in 1929, the Brewster Recreation Center was Joe Louis' training headquarters during his amateur boxing career in the early 1930s. He won the 1934 Detroit Golden Gloves and the National A.A.U. title training at Brewster.

Renamed the Brewster-Wheeler Recreation Center in 1969, the historic landmark closed its doors in 2006 but was saved from demolition through community fundraising. It reopened in 2016 as a community center with restaurants, retail stores and residential units.

Joe Louis

As a stable-mate of Eddie Futch, Joe Louis won the 1934 National Light-heavyweight Golden Gloves and turned professional the same year. Known as the "Brown Bomber," Louis captured the World Heavyweight Championship in 1937 against James J. Braddock and held it until 1949. Joe Louis retired in 1951 with a professional career mark of 66-3-0 (52 KO's).

Louis' title reign of 12 years with 25 successful title defenses is still a record. Louis is ranked as the #1 heavyweight of all-time by the International Boxing Research Organization, and ranked #1 on The Ring Magazine's list of the 100 Greatest Punchers of All-Time. He was inducted into the International Boxing Hall of Fame in 1990.

Jack Blackburn

Joe Louis' trainer, Jack Blackburn, was an outstanding lightweight boxer in the early part of the 20th century. He fought some of the legendary fighters of his era in all weight classes including Joe Gans, Sam Langford, Harry Greb, Gunboat Smith and Philadelphia Jack O'Brien. Blackburn retired from professional boxing in 1923 to become a trainer. His professional ring record was 46-9-12 (33 KOs).

After guiding Sammy Mandell and Bud Taylor to world titles, Blackburn acquired Joe Louis and sculpted one of the greatest masterpieces in boxing history. He trained the "bomber" for eight years, piloting him to the heavyweight championship and an undefeated title reign before passing away in 1942.

Ray Arcel

As a New York based boxing trainer, Ray Arcel was active from the 1920s through the 1980s. Arcel began his training career at New York's Stillman's Gym and worked with world champions Benny Leonard, Ezzard Charles, Jim Braddock, Barney Ross, Bob Olin, Tony Zale, Billy Soose, Ceferino Garcia, Lou Brouillard, Teddy Yarosz, Freddie Steele, Jackie Kid Berg, Alfonso Frazier, Abe Goldstein, Frankie Genaro, Sixto Escobar, Charley Phil Rosenberg, Larry Holmes and Roberto Duran.

Arcel came out of an eighteen-year retirement in 1972 to work with Durán. He retired again after Durán quit in his "No Mas" fight against Sugar Ray Leonard. At 82-years old, he assisted head trainer Eddie Futch in preparing Larry Holmes for his 1982 successful title defense against Gerry Cooney. Ray Arcel died on March 6, 1994, at the age of 94.

Jimmy Edgar

Jimmy Edgar, out of the Brewster Center in Detroit Michigan, fought as a middleweight from 1940-1947. He had three bouts with the future middleweight champion Jake LaMotta. Edgar retired with a career mark of 35-5-1 (20 KO's). Jimmy Edgar passed away in 1985.

Holman Williams

Holman Williams is considered by many to have been the greatest ring technician that ever lived. Futch cited Williams and Charley Burley as the two greatest fighters he ever had the privilege to see and was quoted as saying that he would rather watch Williams shadow-box than watch most other fighters in action.

Williams scored victories over boxing notables like Steve Belloise, Eddie Booker, Charley Burley, Cocoa Kid, Lloyd Marshall, Archie Moore, Bob Satterfield, and Kid Tunero. In 1946, after nearly 14 years as a pro, he lost back-to-back decisions to Marcel Cerdan and Jake LaMotta.

Williams retired in 1948 with a record of 145-31-11 (35 KO's) After his retirement, Williams helped out as a weekend maintenance man at a youth center in Akron, Ohio. He was killed in a fire that engulfed the club in 1967.

Charley Burley

Charley Burley was one of the great "uncrowned" champions of the 1940s and '50s. Burley was a member of "Black Murderers Row" of middleweight fighters known for their toughness and boxing ability. "Black Murderers Row," coined by writer Budd Schulberg, included Holman Williams, Lloyd Marshal, Jack Chase and "Coco Kid." These fighters were never given a chance to fight for the title.

Charlie Burley was considered the best among this group and the best all-around fighter who never competed for a championship. Burley fought most of the top contenders of his era and along the way, defeated future world champions Billy Soose, Archie Moore and Fritzie Zivic.

Never stopped in 98 professional fights, Charley Burley retired in 1950 with a ring record of 83-12-2 (50 KO's). Charley Burley was voted into the Ring Hall of Fame (1982), World Boxing Hall of Fame (1987) and the International Boxing Hall of Fame (1992).

Henry Armstrong

In 1937, Armstrong KO'd Petey Sarron to win the World Featherweight Championship and was named "Fighter of the Year" by the Ring magazine. The following year, Armstrong defeated Barney Ross by a fifteen-round unanimous decision to win the World Welterweight Championship and then defeated Lou Ambers by a fifteen-round split-decision to win the World Lightweight Championship.

Armstrong was the only boxer in history to hold world titles in three separate weight divisions simultaneously, and all three titles were undisputed championships. After Armstrong turned the trick in 1938, no professional boxer could hold titles in more than one weight class at a time.

In 1940, Armstrong fought Ceferino Garcia (whom he has previously defeated) to a draw for a portion of the World Middleweight Championship. A victory would have given Armstrong a fourth divisional title in an era with only eight weight divisions. Armstrong retired from the ring with a record of 151-21-9 (101 KO's)

Henry Armstrong defended the World Welterweight Championship a division record 19 times. Armstrong was voted into the International Boxing Hall of Fame (1990), voted by Ring Magazine #2 of the "80 Best Fighters of the Past 80 Years" (2002), and ranked #2 in Bert Sugar's "Boxing's Greatest Fighters" (2006). Armstrong died in Los Angeles in 1988.

Barry Gordy

Working with Eddie Futch, Gordy launched his pro boxing career in 1947 with a points win over Frankie Branchetti. Once fighting on the same card as the "Brown Bomber" Joe Louis, Gordy continued boxing until he was drafted in the U.S. Army during the Korean War in 1950. His career mark was 12-3-2 (5 KO's).

After his release from the Army, Gordy decided to concentrate his efforts on songwriting and opened a record shop in Detroit. In 1956, Gordy wrote a song entitled "Reet Petite" that became a hit for Jackie Wilson and launched his music career. After penning a string of hits for Wiilson and Etta James including "Lonely Teardrops," Berry formed his own label, Tamla records, and opened his Detroit recording studio "Hitsville U.S.A."

In 1960, he consolidated his recording and music publishing under the banner of Motown Records Corporation. Before long, he had the Supremes, Smokie Robinson & The Miracles, Temptations and Stevie Wonder signed to the Motown label. Motown continued to produce mega-hits throughout the 1960s and '70s and was sold to MCA in 1988 for $61 million dollars. Gordy remained indebted to Eddie Futch for the work ethic he taught him as a young man. Berry Gordy was inducted into the *Rock and Roll Hall of Fame in* 1988.

Don Jordon

Futch's first world champion, Don Jordan, captured the welterweight title in December 1958 against Virgil Akins.

Jordon won the rematch against Akins in '59 and lost his welterweight crown to Benny "Kid' Paret in 1960. Don Jordon retired from boxing in 1962 with a record of 51-23-1 (17 KO's). Don Jordon died in 1997.

Ali v. Frazier: "Fight of the Century"

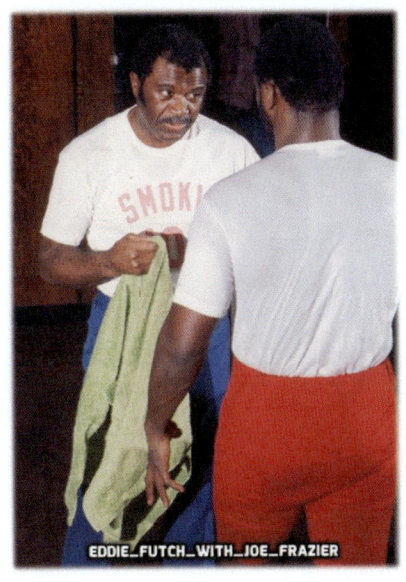

Futch's development of Frazier into a bob-and-weave fighter worked to nullify Ali's great timing and lightning quick hand speed. Joe's continuous head movement offered an elusive target for Ali and enabled Frazier to slip punches and get inside of Ali's defense. Futch also recognized that when Ali threw an uppercut, he stood straight up leaving an opening for Frazier's punishing left hook.

Futch's game plan was simple. Cut off the ring and back Ali into the ropes. Work the body, then the head. Follow Ali's right uppercuts with left hooks. Ali, taken out of his fight-plan was staggered in the 11th round, and floored in the 15th. Frazier won the decision and retained his heavyweight title. It was the beginning of the greatest trilogy and heavyweight boxing history.

Ali v. Frazier III: "Thrilla in Manila"

The "Thrilla in Manila" was the third and final installment of the Ali-Frazier trilogy. Dethroned by Foreman in '73, Frazier lost his non-title rematch with Ali the following year.

"The Greatest" in turn, did what no man had ever done; "rope-a-doped" the crown off of "Big George" Foreman in the "Rumble in the Jungle" and regained the heavyweight championship. With Frazier as the number-one contender, the 1975 "Thrilla in Manila" was born.

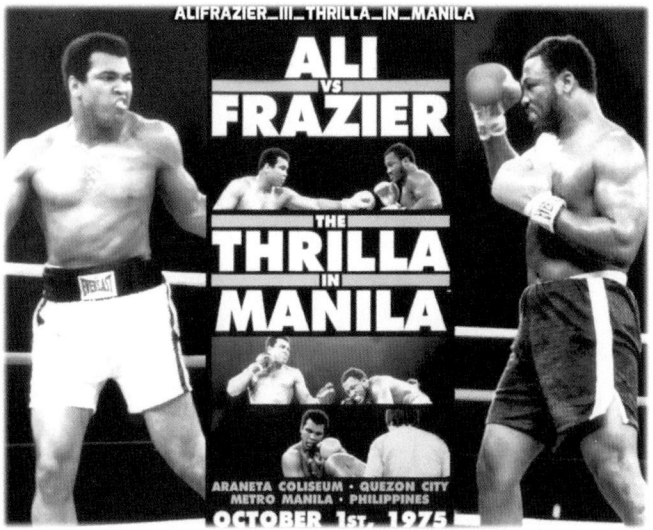

Futch employed the same strategy with Joe he had in their first two encounters with Ali, with Frazier applying constant pressure and fire power. Although both fighters were past their prime, the Manila bout is considered one of the most spectacular, action-packed heavyweight contests of all time.

After fourteen, grueling, non-stop, action packed rounds, Futch realized that Frazier's was nearly blind from eye swelling and couldn't defend himself against Ali's punching speed and power. Rather than risk permanent eye damage, Futch made the courageous decision to stop the fight and call an end to one of the greatest boxing match-ups of all time.

Although Frazier briefly protested the stoppage, Futch said confidently, "it's all over Joe. No one will ever forget what you did here today." In some ways, Futch's act of surrender, said more about the character of this great trainer than all of his victories combined.

Ring magazine picked "Thrilla in Manila" as "Fight of the Year" (1975) and #1 "Fight of All Time" (1996). ESPN's Sports Century ranked the fight, the fifth greatest sporting event of all-time (1996).

Joe Frazier

After winning the Gold Medal at the 1964 Tokyo Olympic Games, Joe Frazier launched his professional boxing career the following year under the guidance of Yancey "Yank" Durham. Frazier remained undefeated though the decade, beating the top contenders of the era including Doug Jones, George Chuvalo, Oscar Bonavena and Jerry Quarry.

When Heavyweight Champion Muhammad Ali was exiled from the sport in 1967, a WBA elimination tournament was held to find his successor. In the finals, Frazier was matched with Buster Mathis for the New York State World Championship. On March 4, 1968, Smokin' Joe KO'd Mathis in the 14th round to win the title.

After defending his crown against Mando Ramos, Oscar Bonavena and Jerry Quarry, Frazier was 24-0 and voted "Fighter of the Year" for 1969. The following year, Frazier stopped Jimmy Ellis in four rounds to capture the "undisputed" World Heavyweight Championship.

With Ali's license reinstated in 1970, the "Fight of the Century" was set for the following year. It would be the first time, two unbeaten fighters would meet for the heavyweight championship. Under the guidance of Durham and Futch, Smokin' Joe retained his title with a 15-round unanimous decision.

Joe Frazier v. George Foreman

Frazier's championship reign ended in January 1973, against George Foreman. "Big George" dropped Frazier six times before the fight was stopped in the second round. In January 1974, Frazier lost a unanimous decision in his non-title rematch against Ali. Later that year, Ali regained his heavyweight crown by defeating George Foreman in the "Rumble in the Jungle."

The highly anticipated Ali-Frazier rubber-match, "The Thrilla in Manila," was one of the hardest fought boxing contests of all time. Ali retained the championship when Eddie Futch stopped the bout in the 14th round to keep Frazier from permanent eye injury. Ali would later admit, "it was like death, closest thing to dying that I know of."

In 1976, at the age of 32, Frazier retired. After a one fight comeback in 1981, Frazier exited the sport with a professional record of 32-4-1 (27 KO's). Joe Frazier passed away at his home in Philadelphia on November 7, 2011.

Ken Norton

Ken Norton began his boxing career in 1963 as a U.S. Marine and won the All-Marine Heavyweight Championship, three years in a row. He turned professional in 1967 and began training under the guidance of Eddie Futch the following year. Norton went 16-0 before losing his first boxing match to Jose Luis Garcia by KO in 1970.

Norton remained undefeated for the next three years and faced Muhammad Ali for the NABF Heavyweight Championship in March 1973, winning the 12-round split-decision. Norton credited Eddie Futch's ring strategy for his success. After losing his rematch with Ali six months later, Norton challenged George Foreman for the W.B.C. and W.B.A. heavyweight championship and lost via knockout in the second round.

Norton remained unbeaten until September 1976, when he challenged Muhammad Ali for the WBC and WBA World Heavyweight Championships at Yankee Stadium. Norton lost the hard fought 15-round "rubber match" by unanimous decision.

When Norton beat Jimmy Young in a heavyweight elimination tournament, he moved into the number-one position for the title. After Leon Spinks defeated Muhammad Ali for the heavyweight championship and refused to defend against Norton in his first title defense, Norton was awarded the World Heavyweight Championship.

Norton lost the crown in his first title defense against Larry Holmes in 1978. Ken Norton continued fighting until 1982 and retired with a record of 42-7-1 (32 KO's). Ken Norton was awarded "Fighter of the Year" by the Boxing writers Association (1977) and inducted into the World Boxing Hall of Fame (1989) and the International Boxing Hall of Fame (1992). Ken Norton passed away September 13, 2013.

Alexis Arguello

Born in Managua, Nicaragua in 1953, Alexis Arguello made his professional boxing debut in 1968. He stopped Ruben Olivares in thirteen rounds to win the WBA Featherweight Championship on November 23, 1974. He won the WBC Super-Featherweight Championship with a thirteenth-round TKO of Alfredo Escalera in 1978.

Arguello moved up to the Lightweight class and in 1981 took the WBC Lightweight Championship with a fifteen-round unanimous decision against Jim Watt. After four title defenses at lightweight, Arguello attempted to make history by becoming the first boxer to capture world titles in four weight classes.

In November 1982, Alexis challenged Aaron "The Hawk" Pryor for his Light- Welterweight title and lost the bout by TKO in the 14th round. Ring Magazine named the Pryor vs. Arguello bout "Fight of the Decade" and the eighth greatest title fight of all-time. In the 1983 rematch, Arguello lost by a tenth-round kayo. After a brief comeback, Alexis Arguello retired in 1995 with a ring record of 77-8-0 (62 KOs).

Alexis was inducted into the International Boxing Hall of Fame (1992) and voted by The Ring magazine as the "Greatest Junior-Lightweight of All Time (1994). Alexis Arguello died in Managua, Nicaragua on July 1, 2009 from a self-Inflicted gunshot wound to the chest.

Bobby Chacon

"Schoolboy" Bobby Chacon started boxing professionally in 1972 and won his first 19 fights. After defeating former world bantamweight champion, Jesus "Chucho" Castillo, Chacon challenged Mexican legend, Ruban Olivares, for the NABF Featherweight title and lost by a technical decision.

In 1975, after five consecutive wins including the defeat of future champion Danny "Little Red" Lopez, Chacon beat Alfredo Marcano to capture the WBC World Featherweight Championship with a 9th round TKO. After one title defense, he lost his crown to Ruben Olivares.

Chacon beat Olivares in their 1977 non-title rubber-match via 10-round unanimous decision. Two years later, Chacon squared off against Rafael "Bazooka" Limon's for his NABF Super-Featherweight title and fought to a draw.

In November of 1979, Chacon challenged ring legend Alexia Arguello for the WBC World Super-Featherweight crown and lost via referees decision in the 7th round. After losing in another title bid against Cornelius "Boza" Edwards in 1981, Chacon put together an impressive string of five consecutive victories.

In December 1982, Bobby again challenged Rafael "Bazooka" Limon; this time for his WBC Super-Featherweight World title. In one of the greatest ring battles of all time, Chacon came out the winner over the 15-round distance. The Ring Magazine elected the bout "Fight of the Year" (1982).

Chacon won his rematch with Boza-Edwards with a 12-round unanimous decision. Ring Magazine voted the Chacon-Boza-Edwards contest, "Fight of the Year" (1983). Attempting to become a three-division champion, Bobby moved up in weight and challenged Ray "Boom Boom" Mancini for his world lightweight crown and lost by a 3rd round TKO.

Chacon continued boxing until 1988, retiring from the sport with a ring record of 59-7-1 (49 KOs). Bobby Chacon was inducted into the International Boxing Hall of Fame in 2005. Bobby Chacon died in California, September 7, 2016 at the age of 64.

Ruben Olivares

One of the greatest boxing champions in Mexican history, Ruben "El Puas" Olivares dominated the bantamweight and featherweight divisions for nearly a decade. A power puncher with a devastating left hook, Olivares racked up 79 KO wins in his boxing career.

Olivares stopped Lionel Rose in 1969 to win the WBC and WBA World Bantamweight Championship and extend his winning streak to 54-0 with 49 knockouts. The following year he made two title defenses before losing via TKO to Jesus "Chucho" Castillo.

In his 1971 rematch with Castillo, Olivares regained the World Bantamweight Championship by unanimous decision then lost the following year in his third title defense against Rafael Herrera.

In 1973, Olivares moved up to the featherweight class and won the NABF crown by beating, then undefeated, Bobby Chacon. In July 1974, Olivares took the WBA World Featherweight Championship crown from Zensuke Utagawa with a 7th round KO. In his first title defense, Olivares lost his championship to Latin sensation and future Eddie Futch protégé, Alexis Arguello.

In his second meeting with Chacon, Olivares regained the World Featherweight Championship with a 2nd round KO. His featherweight reign was short-lived though when he was upset by David Kotey in his first title defense.

Ruben's last pro fight was in 1988 and he retired with an amazing record of 88-13-3 (79 KO's). His knockout winning streaks of 22 and 21 in a row are the two longest in the history of boxing. Olivares was inducted into the International Boxing Hall of Fame (1991) and voted "Bantamweight Fighter of the Century" by the Associated Press (1999).

Larry Holmes v. Michael Spinks

As head trainer to both Holmes and Spinks, Futch stepped away from this historic bout. Futch said his decision not to be involved in the contest cost him roughly $750,000 but added, "some things are more important than money.

Though undefeated as a professional fighter, Spinks, was a 6-1 underdog attempting to become the first reigning World Light-heavyweight Boxing Champion to win the heavyweight title. Not an easy task considering nine times throughout history, other light-heavyweight champs have attempted the same feat and failed. Georges Carpentier, Tommy Lochran, Billy Conn, Archie Moore and Bob Foster are just of few of the legendary champions that tried.

Undefeated Heavyweight champion Larry Holmes, with a record of 48-0, was attempting to accomplish another "first" in the sport. A Holmes victory would tie Rocky Marciano's long-standing ring record of 49-0. Holmes plan was to defeat Spinks and win a subsequent bout and retire as the first heavyweight champion in history with a perfect record of 50-0-0.

The "Spinks Jinx" ended Larry Holmes dream of an undefeated career. Spinks strategy to keep jabbing and moving, worked effectively in negating Holmes rhythm, and heavyweight power. Ring Magazine voted the Holmes-Spinks fight "Upset Fight of the Year" (1985).

Riddick Bowe

After winning the Silver Medal against Lennox Lewis at the 1988 Seoul Olympic Games, Futch took Riddick Bowe under his wing and created a heavyweight champion. Agreeing to train hard and follow Futch's game plan, Bowe went on the win the World Heavyweight Championship with a victory over Evander Holyfield in 1992. After two title defenses, Bowe lost his crown by decision in his rematch with Holyfield. Futch continued to train Bowe as champion until 1996 when he dropped him for 'not listening.' "Big Daddy" Bowe retired from boxing in 2008 with a record of 43-1-0.

Evander Holyfield v. Lennox Lewis

In March 1999, the Holyfield-Lewis match was finally held and billed as the "Undisputed" Heavyweight Championship of the World. Lennox Lewis dominated the 12-round affair, though it ended in a highly controversial draw.

Lennox Lewis v. Riddick Bowe

Unfortunately, the highly anticipated Olympic Games heavyweight rematch never took place. After Bowe won the World Heavyweight Championship against Evander Holyfield, he chose to defend it against it a fading Michael Dokes and top contender, Jesse Ferguson. Bowe infamously tossed his W.B.C. Championship Belt into the trash can at a London press conference, surrendering his championship in lieu of defending against Lewis.

Later HBO stepped up and offered 32-million dollars to make the Bowe-Lewis fight, still it never came off. A winner-take-all" scenario was proposed by Bowe's manager Rock Newman, but when the deal was accepted by the Lewis camp, it was disregarded by team Bowe.

In June '94, a tentative agreement was reached for a Lewis-Bowe showdown after Lewis' mandatory title defense against Oliver McCall. Unfortunately for Bowe, McCall knocked Lewis out and the dream match was never made.

Lewis would regain the WBC heavyweight championship in his 1997 rematch with McCall and continued to defend his title against the best fighters of his era before retiring from the sport in 2002.

George Foreman vs. Tommy Morrison

The Foreman-Morrison bout was for the vacated WBO Heavyweight Championship. The 44-years old Foreman was trying to become the oldest heavyweight champion in history. A win for the 24-year old Morrison would guarantee him a lucrative title shot against WBC champion Lennox Lewis. Morrison beat Foreman by a unanimous 12-round decision.

Morrison lost his WBO title in his tune-up defense against journeyman Michael Bentt along with his 7.5 million dollar contract against Lennox Lewis. He would not have the opportunity to fight Lennox Lewis for another two and a half years and lose by 6th round TKO.

Tommy "The Duke" Morrison

Tommy Morrison made his professional boxing debut in 1988 and racked up 28 straight victories before losing to Ray Mercer by kayo for the WBO Heavyweight Championship in 1991.

In 1993, Tommy Morrison won the WBO Heavyweight title against George Foreman and lost it against Michael Bentt the same year. Two years later, Morrison defeated Donovan "Razor" Ruddick for the vacant IBC Heavyweight Championship and lost it in his first title defense against Lennox Lewis.

After being diagnosed with the HIV virus in 1995, Morrison beat Marcus Rode in Tokyo, Japan and retired. He made a brief comeback in 2007 winning two fights before retiring for good the following year with a career mark of 48-3-1 (42 KO's). Tommy Morrison died on September 1, 2003 at the age of 44.

"Iron" Mike Tyson

Mike Tyson served less than three years of a six-year sentence for a rape conviction and was paroled in March 1995. Resuming his fight career, Iron Mike was matched with journeyman Peter McNeely and won via disqualification in the first round. The Tyson-McNeely bout grossed close to $100-million dollars, setting an all-time record in PPV sales.

In 1996, Tyson regained the WBC version of the heavyweight championship with a third round TKO victory over British champion, Frank Bruno. No. 1 contender Lennox Lewis turned down a $13.5 million guarantee to meet Tyson, but accepted $4 million to step aside and allow Tyson to challenge WBC champion Bruce Seldon. Tyson scored a first round TKO and regained the heavyweights championship.

In his first WBC title defense, Tyson was matched with era rival, Evander Holyfield on November 11, 1996. In one of the most shocking upsets in heavyweight history, Holyfield dominated the previously unbeatable Iron Mike, stopping him by TKO in round 11.

The Tyson-Holyfield rematch was one of the most bazaar exhibitions of strange behavior in heavyweight boxing history. The bout proved to be more controversial that their first meeting. The fight was stopped in the third round with Tyson disqualified for biting Holyfield on both ears. Tyson claimed it was retaliation for Holyfield's constant head butting.

Tyson continued his boxing career against second rate fighters until he was eventually matched with WBC, IBF and IBO heavyweight champion Lennox Lewis in 2002. In the first defense of his title, Lewis dominated Tyson throughout the fight and won the bout by knock out in the eighth round. This fight was the highest-grossing event in pay-per-view history at that time, generating $106.9 million in buys.

After the Lewis bout, Mike continued his career until June 11, 2005, when he stunned the boxing world by quitting before the start of the seventh round in a close bout against journeyman Kevin McBride. He later claimed he took the fight for the money and had lost his interest in the sport. "Iron" Mike Tyson retired from professional boxing with a career mark of 50-6-0 (44 KO).

About the Author

F. Daniel Somrack was born in Cleveland, Ohio. His first recollections of boxing were of watching *Gilette's Friday Night Fights* with his Father Frank, who had been an amateur boxer in the U.S. Navy during WWII. Frank fought for the heavyweight championship at Navy Pier Chicago in 1942, under the guidance of world lightweight contender Davey Day and world light-heavyweight champion Anton Christoforidis.

Many of Dan's childhood afternoons were spent at the neighborhood Maxim's Pizzaeia, owned by former World Light-Heavyweight Champion Joey Maxim and his brother Manny. The walls of the store were lined with photos of Maxim in his classic ring battles against boxing legends like Archie Moore and Sugar Ray Robinson. Joey Maxim's red championship gloves were mounted in a frame.

A high-school pastime of Dan's was watching classic fight films on 16mm borrowed from the local library. Classic bouts like Johnson-Ketchel, Johnson - Jeffries, Johnson -Willard, Dempsey-Willard, Dempsey-Tunney, Louis-Schmeling, Marciano-Walcott and others.

When Muhammad Ali came to Cleveland to defend his heavyweight championship against the Bayonne Bleeder" Chuck Wepner, Dan was there. He met his childhood idol Muhammad Ali at the pre-fight press conference along with Ali's sparring partner and future heavyweight champion Larry Holmes. The Ali-Wepner fight was the inspiration behind Sylvester Stallone's " Rocky" franchise.

Los Angeles, California

DAN_SOMRACK_WITH_CHAMPIONS_FOREVER__ALI__FRAZIER_A

In 1985, Dan relocated to Los Angeles to work in the film industry. While producing several low-budget feature films with First American Film Capital, he was approached by an investment group willing to fund a documentary about Muhammad Ali. With the help of Ali's good pal and photographer, Howard Bingham, the show came together.

When Joe Frazier, Larry Holmes, George Foreman and Ken Norton came on board, *Champions Forever* was born. Dan served as the Supervising Producer and Story Consultant on the film that was released in 1989. *Champions Forever* went on to become the highest-selling, original sports documentary of the era.

Dan went on to Co-Produce *Latin Legends of Boxing* starring Alexis Arguello, Julio Cesar Chavez, Kid Gavilan, Carlos Ortiz, Salvador Sanchez and Roberto Duran. He also worked with former world welterweight champion Carlos Palomino who served as the Associate Producer. The film was shot on location in Panama, Nicaragua, Costa Rica, Miami and New York.

In 1993, Somrack went to Las Vegas, Nevada and conducted a one-on-one interview with legendary trainer Eddie Futch. Futch went all the way back in the sport to the 1930s beginning at the Brewster Center in Detroit with heavyweight champion, Joe Louis. This interview's transcription was the basis for *The Eddie Futch Interview*.

Havana, Cuba

In the mid-1990s, Dan traveled to Havana, Cuba and met the great Olympic boxing champion Teofilo Stevenson. Over the years, he became a frequent visitor to the island nation and forged a close relationship with the Cuban sports hero. Dan has a profile article published about Teofilo Stevenson entitled *The Cuban Legend* that appeared in the Spring 2000 issue of Smoke Magazine.

In 2005, F. Daniel Somrack authored *Boxing in San Francisco* for Arcadia Publishing. The book covers the period between 1890-1914 when San Francisco was the Mecca of boxing on the west coast. The greatest champions of the era battled in the city including Jack Johnson, Stanley Ketchel, James J. Jeffries, James J. Corbett and Abe Attell.

F. Daniel Somrack continues to write and publish profile stories on boxing legends from around the world. His most recent works *Jack Dempsey: The Nonpareil and Pancho Villa: The Filipino Legend can be found* on Amazon Kindle Books.

Printed in Great Britain
by Amazon